A Guide to the C

~

How to Build a
Stone Wall

~

by
Hunter Adair

Robson Print Ltd.
Hexham, Northumberland
www.robsonprint.co.uk

nfucountryside

This is to certify that

Hunter Adair

*was a runner-up in
the Countryperson Of The Year
category at the 2002
NFU Countryside Awards*

nfucountryside

Ian Dalzell
Chief Executive
NFU Countryside

Sponsored by

A curlew sitting on four eggs . . . they come to the moors and farms every Spring to nest. Sometimes close to Stone Walls

INTRODUCTION

I have lived and worked in the countryside all my life and have studied many species of wildlife, plants and stone walls which are fascinating. There is something to see and learn every day in the countryside.

The countryside is now visited by more and more people every year from all walks of life.

Many more people are now concerned with the countryside and the environment which we live in and question many of the decisions that ar proposed to alter the countryside.

Some people think the countryside is being spoiled and that some of the wild animals, birds and plants will disappear for ever.

Wild animals and birds adapt very easily to different environments. They have to in order to survive and they do it well. Foxes for instance have adapted to live in the cites. There are many things in the countryside to see and use if you know roughly what to look for and where to find them.

The general public don't often get the opportunity to visit the farms near to them, although a number of farms have now opened their gates up the general public. This gives more people a look at how the countryside is managed.

Some farmers have really set their farms out to try and show the public as much as possible how they look after the countryside and its wildlife.

This is the first in a series of small books to be published from the manuscript A Guide To The Countryside and is about Stone Walls, how and why this pattern of stone walls were constructed in our countryside.

How to Build A Stone Wall

STONE WALLS

Conservation of the country's heritage is of great interest at present, with so many different organisations and groups being set up to preserve and look after many of the old buildings, parks, woodlands, monuments and many other interesting sites which cover the land.

The farmers landlords and organisations look after the countryside very well. The countryside we live in today only looks the way we see it because many farmers and landowners have looked after the countryside for countless generations using good farming practice's which have been passed down from father to son.

There are many stone walls and stone buildings in the countryside which catch your eye as you pass by. The stone walls have been built by craftsmen over many generations. Many visitors to the countryside and the Dales are attracted and puzzled by the miles and miles of stone walls which sneak up the hillsides and disappear into the distance over the highest hills.

A small hole at the base of the stone wall to let water pass through is known as a "Water Smoot"

Constructing a stone wall, note the rubble in the middle

The stones going through the wall are known as Tiebands, Through
Stones or Thrusts

When was this pattern of stone walls constructed on our countryside? Who built the walls? Why and how? These are some of the questions that one hears not only from the occasional visitor, but also from some Dales born and bred people as well.

The main object in building the drystone walls was to provide a fence to keep different types of stock separated and also provide a dividing line between farms and estates. The reason the walls were built dry was because it was too expensive to transport lime, sand and water up the hillsides.

The stones to build the walls out on the high hills had to be quarried locally, in fact this was done by digging out the rocks as near as possible. the digging would be moved as the wall progressed, where the rocks were quarried can be seen on some hills where there are walls.

Hares boxing

The stones had to be carried by 'slipe' (sledge) and horse to the wall, this was by no means an easy task as there were roughly a good tone of stone to every yard (0.91m) of wall. The wall would be built to a height of 4 foot 6 inches (1.37m), to the coping, or topping stone which is the top stone on the wall. The walls vary a great deal in height from 4 foot (1.21m) to 6 foot (1.82m).

There are many single stone walls built with round stones, which were stones collected from arable land, or river beds and due to wear and tear the edges of the stones have become rounded. Many single stone walls have been standing since the last century and longer, and some of these walls are quite easily damaged.

The early stone walls were an ancient art, which were built by good craftsmen. The Troutbeck Painable Fence Book, first written in 1680, records that the fences and stone walls for which the town was responsible and allocated each man's responsibility for a stated section of wall.

The Troutbeck Jury saw to it that every tenant maintained his painable fences or they would be in pain, that was, fined six shillings and eight pennies (33 pence).

A side view of a stone wall being built, note the stones going through the wall

A stone wall in the north with large stones placed in the wall

The stone built church at Falstone in Northumberland

DATING STONE WALLS

Dating a stone wall is vry difficult, because walls don't have any date stones, although many old buildings do have date stones somewhere on them. In some cases wall plants might provide some clues as to the age of a wall, as some local plant species maybe found which were more common and abundant long before changes were made to the ground cover.

Some of the oldest walls are usually built with an unsorted amount of clearance stones and builders, sometimes they include some very large stones. The oldest walls in Western Britain are likely to be clearance walls which formed fields around farmsteads. Some of these oldest walls seemed to be haphazardly built and often changed direction to include some large boulders, or to avoid rivers and streams, or various other obstacles.

The old Blacksmith's Shop at Muggleswick

Sometimes various objects have been found in some old stone walls, which may also give a clue as to when the wall was built. The bowls of broken clay pipes have been found frequently in some old walls. Whenever such clues are used to date a wall, they may only however simply represent later additions or repairs that have been made to the original wall.

A most extraordinary article was found in a wall at Treswithian, Camborne in Cornwall, it was a hunting horn, thought to be from either te 17th or 18th century and is recorded to mark the site of a fatal hunting accident in the late 18th century. Again the horn may have been placed in the wall when the wall was being repaired, rather than in the original construction, usually the stones themselves are all there is to go on, with any written records which are available.

The old Lead Mine at Killhope in Co. Durham

Finding things in old stone walls brings to my mind about a pair of English pistols which were found in a box, in the stone wall of an old farm house in Northumberland when the house was being renovated.

The pistols could be dated as the makers name was stamped on them, but this does not mean to say the farm house was built when the pistols were put in the wall, they could have been hidden in the wall long after the house was built. It however does give some clue to how old the house may be.

Stone walls built near to old villages, farmsteadings, or to some habitation sites which may now be abandoned, are most likely to be older than walls which were built further away from habitation. Many stone walls which were

The late Bill Thompson with his sons Billy and John at Thornbrough Quarry

A stone wall being built at Slaley

Rabbits often hide and shelter in the stone walls

Hares many times shelter close to the stone walls

The curlew often nests out on the hills and moors in the spring and any
stone walls nearby can be of great shelter to the young chicks

Many farm buildings are built entirely with stone

Farmers and friends in the heart of the stone wall country near Hexham

built out on the hilltops, or on out-by land, are likely to have been built after the Enclosure Act of 1801 and will be easier to date.

Many times when I am out walking with my dogs in the various woods I come across some old parts of stone walls which had been in use long before the trees were planted. There are probably records of when the trees were planted as many of the trees I see are of soft wood, such as fir and spruce and can't be much older than forty years or so.

Stone walls attract stoats which hunt in and out of the stone walls for mice and rabbits

Inspecting some of these broken down walls I find many of them are just singe walls and seem to be bult with quarried stone rather than clearance stones. Some of these walls are more likely to have been built as stock fencing which were near to the farmsteads.

Many of the old stone walls are as dry as can be and are very often blown full of leaves, some walls out on the hills are often filled with old grass. There is ample warmth in these old walls for many small animals, such as mice, weasels and rabbits and they provide good shelter on a stormy day.

The Act of Parliament of 1801, which is known as the Enclosure Act empowered commissioners to survey the lands to be enclosed by stone walls.

Old farm buildings in the north.
Note the large stone slates

Most of the stone walls in the Lake District were built following this Act of 1801.

DISTRICT WALLS

In the north of England, in the Northumberland and Durham area, three types of stone were used to build the stone walls, Sandstone, Limestone and Whinstone. Many walls south of the river Tyne are built with Sandstone and in some parts of the north Tyne many walls are built with Whinstone. In the Durham Dales you will find many stone walls built with Limestone. There is a great variety of stone to be found in the north.

The Kestrel hunting for mice and voles

When you travel into south-west Scotland in the Galloway district, you will not be far away from stone walls, or dykes as they are called. They wind up and across the open hills and fit like patchwork and drop down almost into deep gullies. Many walls form a patchwork of small enclosures patterns making little fields and pens which are formed around many small farmsteads.

Many of these Galloway dykes are something of which the district is very proud. 'Galloway dykes' are known wherever man has learnt to build one stone on top of another to make a stockproof dyke.

Otterburn Mill with its lovely old stone buildings started out as a corn mill around 1245. When the mill was first used for cleaning and thickening cloth is not certain but as late as 1914 long after the mill was a working woollen mill farmers were still bringing grain to the mill to be crushed

Otterburn Mill continued to produce cloth until 1977 when the competition from man-made fibres forced it to close. The new owner of the mill has highlighted the hidden treasures of the mill and has also provided a mill shop and a weavers restaurant. The mill is open all year round and is really worth a visit and the food is just great.

The heart of the wall being filled with small packing stones

The Galloway dyke construction is designed to fence in sheep. the soil forthe foundation of the dyke is dug out about four inches (100mm), and a big flat stone is then laid on this foundation or footing stone, the dyke is then built up on two sides and the space between them is filled with small 'hearting stones' which are packed tight.

The marsh thistle is a tall plant with winged stems and narrow leaves with deep crimson flowers confined mainly to wet places

These walls are mainly built to turn sheep and they are slightly different from other stone walls. They have one or two rows of throughstones which go right through the wall plus a 'coverband stone' which is a flat stone laid below the coping stone which is the top stone on the wall. These flat throughstones project about 2 inches (50mm) from the wall face and along with the coping stone, they help to stop the sheep from attempting to jump the wall.

This type of stone wall in Scotland is known as a 'double dyke' because it has two faces which are packed in the middle with small stones or (fillings), much the same as other double dry stone walls. The 'coverband stone' is the only difference, although some stone walls in the Durham Dales

Parts of a stone wall in Galloway, Scotland constructed with round rough stones probably collected from the fields or river beds

have a row of turf put on top of the wall before the top coping stone is laid on, the coping stone forms the wall crown.

The coping stones or copes on Galloway stone walls are placed straight up and down to deter sheep and cattle from nosing at the dyke. The copes are packed so tight they do not move, even though not an ounce of cement has been used in the whole wall structure.

Flat stones laid on top of an old car chassis to make a bridge

Field dykes in Galloway are often built to about a height of 4 foot 6 inches (1.37m) to the coping stone, and 'march' boundary dykes are normally built about a foot higher (1.67m). The stone walls will last a hundred years and more without being touched.

These grey stone dykes in the south-west of Scotland were often rooted in controversy. Durng the time of the Enclosures, much of the open hills and waste lands as they were termed then, were taken over by the landlords who gained the necessary permission in those days.

This robbed the indepedent smallholders of their living, which meant they had to go and work for someone else. The small holders took vengeance againsst the landlords and started pulling down the dykes at night that had been painstakingly built that day. After a time the leaders were caught and the destruction soon stopped.

Stone walls or dykes can be built with any type of stone, but whinstone double dykes are perhaps the most common throughout central Scotland, while sandstone dykes are found in certain districts of southern Scotland and the west coast.

Whinstone is rough and makes a varied and irregular dyke, because much of the stone is (wedge-shaped) which helps to keep each course of the wall level.

Great emphasis is placed when building a stone dyke to 'keep the heart up'. This means keeping the middle of the wall well packed, by placing the filling stones at the same time as the face stones, and by making sure the filling stones are slightly higher than the level of the face stones so that the next course of face stones tips a little down and out towards the outside, which helps the wall to shed water.

The institute of Bankers from Newcastle having a look at part of the Roman Wall

The Church at Hunstanworth on the Durham/Northumberland border

The Lions Rock near Millport in Scotland

The author and two grand children up in the Roman Wall

Some single stone dykes built in the Galloway area are only one stone thick and can be found in and around the Kirkcudbrightshire area where there is granite stone. Some of these single dykes of granite were often built in combination with some double stone dykes to use up the bigger stones.

The rough coarsed-grained granite stones used in building single walls would bind better together with friction and the single walls were better suited to the granite country. Many single dykes are also very common around Dumfriesshire, Argyll and the Western Isles and many of the single walls have no coping stone on them.

A stone wall being built near Haydon Bridge in Northumberland

However, the Roxburgh survey of 1798 recommended a layer of turf be put on the single wall top and the turf was to be placed on its edge and then clapped together with a spade to flatten the turf. The Hebrides survey states that the single stone dykes originated in southern Scotland in 1720 and was generally the best type of dyke for that sheep grazing area.

In the South West of Cornwall, the stone walls or 'Hedges' as they are known in that district, surround the fields and border the roads throughut the whole County and are works of art.

Over the years many farmers in Cornwall will have broken several sets of harrows, had overheated tractors, lost their tempers and spent many hours clearing apparently virgin land of many hidden huge stones and boulders.

In one field in Cornwall, huge pieces of granite a foot thick (0.30m) or more and are as flat as table topes, stand up-ended and side by side for some sixty yards (54m) along one boundary.

Huge stones and boulders have their uses in Cornwall, as the geography and geology of Cornwall doesn't encourage the growth of an abundance of trees, especially along the windswept north coast, so Cornishmen down through the ages have used the local stone to build the walls and hedges that can be seen today.

The stone walls and hedges in Cornwall, not only serve as enclosures for farm stock and as boundaries and borders, but also provide shelter in winter and shade in summer for animals, birds and wildlife. they also act as conservation areas for plants and flowers of all descriptions.

These hedges and walls have many uses. In the walls in a farm yard near Redruth, there are a number of boxes about two foot (0.60m) from the ground which serve as next boxes for the farmer's hens. The farmer unfortunately didn't reap the benefit of his work, as crows, rats and jackdaws found the open nest boxes easy pickings.

Mice like to nest and shelter in the stone walls

This is a true story which happened in Cornwall, one winters day when the children of a country school were at their lessons, a blizzard started and raged around the little school building all day, ceasing only when the time came for the children to go home.

A stone built lime kiln on a Northumberland Farm

The snow however lay thick on the ground covering everything, so heavy was the fall of snow that it was impossible to use or even distinguish the roads and lanes. The children became frightened, thinking they were going to be cut off from their families.

However, the headmaster of the school know of a way to get the children home. He told them to put on their hats and coats, he then led the children out of the school into the white countryside and took them along the tops of the hendges and walls, where the children walked hand in hand safely home.

The stone walls of Wales are constructed with various types of stone, such as granite, limestone, volcanic rocks and slates. The farmsteads on the western foothills of Snowdonia are mainly built with volcanic rock. The stone is tough and coarse and the walls are rough and grey.

In other parts of Wales, you will find stone-faced earth banks rather than free standing stone walls and many times you will find a hedge growing on top of the banks. The stones on the banks are either set vertically, or they are built in a herringbone fashion.

In the areas of Wales where slate has been quarried, you will find slate being used quite a lot on roadside walls, the slate is also used as copings on the wall tops, or you can even find volcanic copings on slate walls.

A stone-built tunnel which once supplied air to a lead mine

Many double-faced walls in Wales are built to a height of 5 feet (1.52m), and although it was once a booming craft in Wales the tendency has been over many years like other parts of the country, for the craft of building stone walls and hedges to by dying out and many of the walls, hedges and stone-faced banks have been left and they have become derelict.

The Lake District walls are built with a variety of different types of stone. Slate is also used a great deal and so is shale and flag stones in many areas. Sandstone, limestone, volcanic rock and granite can all be found in the Lake District walls.

Some walls climb straight up the very steep fell sides and never alter their course. There was a great deal of skill in building these walls as the stones rise by steps and stairs right up the hillsides.

Many walls in the Lake District are built to a height of 4 foot 6 inches (1.37m), although there are walls of various heights. The stone or rock walls are built very similar to the slate walls, although the stone walls are much rougher than the slate walls.

The stone walls around the Carlisle and Kendal area are built mainly with Limestone, and travelling around the Kendal countryside, there are very many narrow country lanes and the grey stone walls are nearly touching your car as you wind your way through the countryside.

As I have already stated many stone walls in the Lake district were built following the Enclosure act of 1801. As the stone walls were built up the very steep hillsides or slopes of the Lakelan fells, the coping stones or cap stones for the walls wre very often rough stones which were lying around, and as some of the hillsides are so steep the coping stones are facing slightly down the hill rather than up the hill to keep the centre of the wall dry, but because of the steep hillsides this puts more pressure on the walls.

THE STONE WALL FEATURES

Although the stone walls, hedges, stone-faced banks and march dykes were all built for a similar purpose, either to separate one man's land from another, or they were built to keep stock separated. Yet these find structures have built into them many other special useful features which are of great interest.

This small rectangular hole at the base of the wall is known as a "Rabbit Smoot" which lets hares and rabbits pass from one pasture to another

One feature of the wall is the coping stone, this is the top stone on the wall which protects the rest of the wall beneath it from the weather. These top stones also have a variety of names, such as cap stones, topping stones, or copes as they are known in Scotland.

The wall coping's can be of turf, stone or slate, some coping stones are dressed and laid side by side on the wall top, other stones are rougher and will lock together with vibration, some coping stones are laid on edge, as some slate coping's are. Some flat stones are also used as coping's which are laid side by side along the length of the wall.

The corncrake likes rough pastures which are many times divided by stone walls

Some coping stones are easily dislodged and sometimes members of the general public remove a coping stone or two from the roadside walls, or from the walls in picnic areas and take them home. When the coping stone is taken from the wall top, the water and snow then gets into the heart of the wall and it starts to detriorate.

Other wall features are the throughstones, these are flat stones which are placed right through the wall and stick out on either side of the wall. Some stone walls only have one row of throughstones, and other walls have two rows of throughstones, depending a great deal on the height of the wall. A double stone wall built to a height of 4 feet 6 inches (1.4m) will probably have two rows of throughstones.

The throughstones are built to stabilise the wall, the throughstones also have other names, such as tiebands, as they are known in Scotland, or

Throughbands. In the north of England I have heard them called Thrusts. the firt row of throughstones is normally laid through the wall about two feet (0.60m) from the wall foundation.

There re also small rectangular holes at the base of some field stone walls, which are known as 'Rabbit Smoots'. These small holes at the base of the stone walls are to let hares and rabbits pass from one pasture to another, they can also be used to drain surface water from one field to another.

These small holes in the walls are also called 'Pop Holes'. In the Durham Dales I once came across an old stone wall on the fell which had a small 8 inch (0.20m) wide stone tunnel which ran alongside the bottom of the wall just under the turf, the tunnel was about 20 yards (18.28m) long. I understand the tunnel was made for rabbits to lie in during the winter months.

There are other larger square or shaped holes at the base of many farm enclosed walls, which allow sheep to pass from one pasture to another. These are also known as Sheep Runs, Cripple Holes, Hogg Holes, or Sheep Smouts, this is just a few of the names they are called.

Grouse in flight

A stone grouse butt near Allenheads in Northumberland

Note how the butt is built with stone and the turf laid on top helps to protect the wall

These sheep holes measure about two feet by two feet (0.60m) by (0.60m) and can be opened and closed at will by placing a tone, or gate across the hole entrance.

The law on boundary fences, dykes, ditches, march dykes, stone faced banks and stone walls, with regards to the game they hold is very complicated.

A number of sportsmen think that if a ditch is on the opposite side of the hendge to the land over which they have the shooting, they have the right to the game and also the right to walk the brow of the ditch.

It is also frequently thought the owner of the hedge or ditch is entitled to four, or six feet of land (1.21m) or (1.82m), from the stub of the hedge.

No man making a ditch can cut into his neighbour's soil, but usually he cuts to the very extremity of his own land. He is of course bound to throw the soil which he digs out onto his own land and if he likes he can plant a hedge on the top of the soil. There is no rule about him being able to claim four or six feet (1.21m) or (1.82m), of land from the stub of the far side of the hedge. A point of law decided upon in 1810 and still stands today.

The grouse blend in well among the heather and their surroundings

As you travel around the countryside in the north of England and into Scotland, you will find small circular stone walls built out on the moors in rows of eight or nine in a row. These are shooting butts, where the guns hide while the beaters with their dogs try and drive the grouse over the butts to the guns.

We call these grouse butts in the north. Some gamekeepers lay turfs flat on top of the stone butts as coping's. I have seen one layer of turf being laid on top of another making the turf about a foot thick (0.30m). The reason turf is used, is to protect the heart of the butts, but most important of all, is so as the shooters sitting in the butts can lay their guns on top of the turf without getting them damaged, or scratched from the stone.

The craftsmen building stone walls or dykes on a regular basis could probably build about a 'Rood' of wall a day, which is seven yards (6.40m). In granite country a 'Rood' will be about six yards (5.48m), the reason for this is because granite is a harder rougher stone to work with. The weather played a good part on the length of wall they built each day.

Some of the old timers at building stone walls often picked up the heaviest hammer nearest to their hand and throw the hammer up the hill as far as they could, they then declared that this was how much wall they were going to build that day.

One of the saddest aspects of many stone walls today is the dereliction of many of these hard won walls, which are either left to decay, or have been bulldozed out of existence. Yet to the hill shepherd and hill sheep, the stone walls are invaluable when a winter blizzard, or the lambing time rains sweep the hills. Many a lamb has suvived because of the stone walls, yet they use no fuels or imports and they are built with natural materials and with skill and hard work.

SHEEP STELLS

Shepherds are people dedicated to the craft of breeding and the general management of sheep. To most of us one sheep looks just like another, but the shepherd every sheep has its own characteristics and the shepherd knows

A Sheep Stell or Sheep Fank where sheep are gathered during stormy weather

A ewe and her lambs

every single one. Some sheep dogs are very clever and are trained to a very high standard. Shepherding is a very skilled job indeed.

There are various strains of sheep bred for the hills such as the Blackface, Swaledale, Cheviot and the Herdwick where in the South you find the Suffolk and South Downs. Some very old breeds of sheep survive in Scotland and the Northern Isles today, notably the Soay Sheep on St. Kilda although there are no longer any pure bred Shetland sheep of the original strain, much of the old breed survives in the present Shetland sheep. Later introductions such as the black-face sheep, Cheviot and Lewis black-face developed as local breeds around the 1760's. The old white-face sheep similar to the Shetland sheep once common throughout Scotland, declined in the face of the new breeds and had vanished by the 1860's.

Large scale sheep farming dates back to the Border Abbeys in the twelfth century, sheep were commn elsewhere and besides the farmers packs or flocks, they were often kept for family purposes. The wool provided clothing and the milk was made into cheese. Ewe milking was carried on in the Borders well into the last century.

One of the main difficulties of sheep husbandry has always been keeping down parasites. At one time sheep were smeared, the fleece was parted in parallel lines and tar or sometimes nicotine was mixed into a greasy paste and rubbed on, this made the fleece difficult to clean when being processed for spinning and dipping was introduced. Early dipping included mixtures of nicotine, soap and sulphur.

Sheep stells or sheep banks of the Border country came in with the Border shepherds and drystone dykes around 1760. Sheep stells are dry stone circular walled buildings built on sheltered parts of the hills where flocks of sheep can be gathered for shelter during stormy weather. The stell walls are around 5 foot high and vary in diameter according to the flock size. Not all stells were built circular, some are square. Most stells in the north are circular. In Ireland some old stone stells were built like a cross and no matter which direction the wind, rain or snow was blowing, cattle or sheep could go into one corner of the cross and find shelter. In the south of England shepherds used to carry gait-hurdles around on the backs, the hurdles were made of woven willow and were very light to carry, they could easily be made up into a pen, the stakes were also light. Sheep could be

The Roe Deer is mainly a woodland animal and often shelters behind the stone walls

The Red Deer roam the hills in herds but in the winter they come down from the heights and many times they take shelter beside a stone wall or rock

gathered near lambing time or to shelter from the wind and rain. The hurdles were sometimes covered with straw or canvas.

With the open hillsides and the common grazing in the crofting counties, the identification of sheep has always been a matter of importance, this was done with lug marks. A pattern was clipped out of one or both ears, each district developed different shapes and combinations. This has now been replaced with the use of dye or branding.

Neat stonework used in farm buildings

Hexham House built in 1723

A Spaniel jumping over a stone wall

47

The Wallace Monument at Burnwiel Farm near Ayr in Scotland